I Never Met a Dog I Didn't Like:

True Entertaining and Educational Stories
About Rescue Dogs and Cats

By Miranda McAdams

AuthorHouse™ LLC
1663 Liberty Drive
Bloomington, IN 47403
www.authorhouse.com
Phone: 1-800-839-8640

Published by AuthorHouse 4/11/2014

ISBN: 978-1-4918-7154-6 (sc)
*   978-1-4918-7155-3 (e)*

Library of Congress Control Number: 2014904407

authorHOUSE®

Introduction

This book is based on the experiences that Miranda McAdams and her husband, Bob, a childless couple, have had as dog and cat rescuers. Over decades, they have saved their own dogs through adoption, and, just this year, entered the world of cat guardianship.

In the past few years, they were one-time foster parents, and have recently participated in the transports of some of their own animals from other states. They also have arranged to drive, transport, and serve as overnight hosts for many other people's animals.

Miranda is grateful that all of their dogs and cats, alive and deceased, were quiet while she wrote and she feels that without their quirky personalities, there would have been no stories to tell.

All of these stories are true and actually happened. Miranda and Bob hope that you and your family enjoy these stories as much as she did writing them and he did taking their pictures.

This book was written for all ages in mind and can be used in the following ways:

a)   By parents when reading bedtime stories to their young children, K-6;

b)   By parents who are teaching their middle school and high school age children to love and respect animals;

c)   By teachers and humane society personnel who are teaching humane education to their students;

d)   By people who are already working in the field of animal rescue;

e)   By people who are new to or about to enter the animal rescue field and who want to know what to expect.

Acknowledgements

This book is dedicated to my grandparents, Marie and Aloysius Sr., who, over the years, took in and fed all sorts of stray and farm animals—dogs, cats, pigs, and a goat--and who served as role models for me as a child on how to treat animals with love and respect.

I want to thank my husband, Bob, for not saying no each time when I've wanted to add a new pet to our family, for taking the wonderful photos of our animals that are included in this book, and for transporting and hosting over-night other people's dogs and other animals on his weekends when he could have been playing with our own animals, puttering around our house, or napping.

I also want to thank our cat experts:

Jennifer I., a driver for a Wisconsin transport group, who brought us Butterscotch, introduced us to the world of cats, and made follow-up visits to Butterscotch;

Janine, Amanda, and Lacey at the Humane Animal Shelter in Greenbush, Wisconsin, who helped us find Gatsby and help him live in harmony with Butterscotch.

Finally, I want to thank the three people responsible for Anton's rescue, life-saving care, and transport. Today he has a stable and loving home due to all of your selfless efforts; it proves that it takes a village to save and raise one animal:

Debbie, Florence Animal Shelter, Anton's foster parent, Anu, and Becky, Transport Coordinator, all in Alabama.

Thank you all!

Miranda McAdams

HOLIDAY LIZZIE

Introduction to Lizzie

Lizzie was a two-year-old buff-colored cocker spaniel who ran away from a Wisconsin puppy mill. She was running loose in the streets one day, when a burly, white-bearded man named Ken, offered her part of his fast food hamburger. She took it gladly and went with Ken back to his house to live with him.

Lizzie went everywhere with Ken on his daily work errands, from his office to city buildings to fast food places, and they quickly became friends; however, a few weeks later, Lizzie was "in the doghouse." Not aware that Lizzie was behind him, Ken fell backwards over her and hurt his back—luckily, Lizzie was unharmed.

After his accident, Ken blamed Lizzie and decided to offer to give her to Bob and Miranda one day while they were meeting with him at his office. They had asked Ken where Lizzie was and he said that she was on his bad list. They were surprised to hear this, but they readily agreed to take her home with them and adopt her. Ken placed Lizzie in Miranda's arms and Miranda held her on her lap while they rode home in the car. They noticed that Lizzie was dirty and had numerous ticks. When they got home, they bathed Lizzie and pulled her ticks and burrs. From that time, they became Lizzie's parents.

Lizzie was one of those smaller dogs who have a huge personality. Even though Lizzie was fearless and acted like she was a queen, she allowed Miranda to dress her up in full costume for the holidays when their other dogs would not stand for even wearing a hat.

Easter Lizzie

Lizzie's first holiday with Miranda and Bob was celebrated on Easter of 1997. They dressed her up in a dress with a cottontail and a bonnet with bunny ears and took her to her favorite dog bakery. Once there, she would bark to announce that she was there and visited with her friend, Sunny, a rescued greyhound, who visited the bakery every Saturday morning. Then Lizzie went behind the bakery counter to smell and see the hot dog biscuits that had just come out of the oven.

Lizzie had discriminating tastes, but she finally selected a warm peanut butter shortbread biscuit. Children and adults alike at the bakery made a big fuss over Lizzie and how cute she looked in her costume. Then Lizzie picked out biscuits for her four pack members and left the bakery to go home. At home, Lizzie found an Easter basket with her name on it. It contained an assortment of dog chews, treats, and colored eggs. Each of her pack members had their own baskets, which did not contain any chocolate, because it would have made them very sick or even die. Lizzie enjoyed her safe treats with her pack members and then went to bed after a day of friends, fun, and celebration.

Halloween Lizzie

Every Halloween, kids and dogs from the neighborhood would descend on Lizzie's house on a Sunday, from 1:00 to 4:00 PM, for treats. Miranda and Bob dressed up Lizzie in her black and orange cape and witch's hat. Lizzie would sit on a chair behind a table that Bob had set up outdoors near the side door of the house. Along with a pumpkin on the table were bowls of little raisin boxes for the kids and dog biscuits for Lizzie to give to any dogs who showed up. Like chocolate, raisins make dogs sick, so Bob had to make sure that none of the dogs who came for trick and treating got a hold of the small raisin boxes that were on the table.

Halloween Witch Lizzie

As children and some dogs showed up in their costumes saying "Trick or Treat," Lizzie would bark to greet them and her four pack members would bark from the inside of the house as well.   A number of children and their parents said that Lizzie looked cute and was well-behaved. The weather was usually cold and Lizzie would be wrapped in a blanket, but Bob and Lizzie would always wait until 4:00 PM to make sure that they didn't miss any of the children, dogs, and parents who were trick-and-treating.

When Lizzie finally came into the house, her pack members were waiting to have their own party with her. Spud, their small black, white, and brown cocker spaniel, was dressed as a pirate without an eye patch; Daisy, their large beige cocker spaniel, wore a white sheet with a hole cut in it for her head to look like a ghost; Gilligana, their black Halden hound, wore a pink tutu as a ballerina; and Maverick, their white and brown beagle-Jack Russell terrier mix was dressed as a cowboy with a western hat and scarf.

For refreshments, everyone had meat-flavored snaps and jerky, because only the humans could eat chocolate. Later they all went to bed tired, but happy.

Santa Lizzie

As Lizzie liked to eat, she became rather plump, so it was no stretch of the imagination for Lizzie to put on a Santa costume, which included a red and white fake fur-lined Santa dress with a hat and black belt, with no beard. On Christmas Eve, Lizzie would wear her Santa Lizzie suit and give out the Christmas presents to their human guests after dinner.

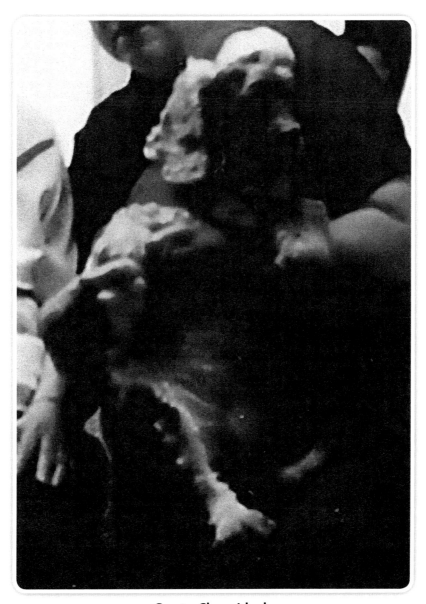

Santa Claus Lizzie

When it came time for Lizzie to hand out gifts to each of her pack members, they tore the wrapping paper off of their edible gifts and started gnawing on them right away. Lizzie opened her gifts, discovering a barbecue bone, a pig ear, and other delicacies. Again, there was no chocolate, because it is poisonous to dogs.

After the guests left, Miranda and Bob and the five dogs went for a walk around the neighborhood to look at the Christmas lights and displays. That night, Santa Lizzie and her pack members went to bed happy and contented to dream about re-chewing the gifts that they had eaten earlier that night.

Conclusion

Lizzie has been gone now for three years, but her holiday dress-up traditions live on with Bob and Miranda's new pack. They try to celebrate every holiday with their dogs if there is a costume and if one of their dogs is willing to wear it.

So far, they have gotten Daisy, their large beige cocker spaniel, to wear a red velvet Valentine's Day dress; Buster, their dark gray shih tzu, to wear a green shamrock costume for St. Patrick's Day; Spud, their small black, white, and brown cocker spaniel, to wear Lizzie's Easter suit and bunny ears; Ashley, their small black cocker spaniel, to wear a flag dress for the 4th of July; and Speedy, their brown beagle, to wear a turkey sweater for Thanksgiving.

Maverick agreed to be their Santa later this year and his photo even appeared in his rescue organization's calendar to raise funds for this rescue group that saved him.

Santa Claus Maverick

LIZZIE DOES HER ERRANDS

Introduction to Lizzie

Our little dog, Lizzie, was a two-year-old buff-colored cocker spaniel who loved to go on errands in the car with people and other dogs. She was a small dog, but she had a big personality. She was fearless and she loved socializing and eating.

Errands Lizzie

Every Saturday, Lizzie spent the whole day going from one place to the next. Wherever Lizzie went with her cute outfits, she brightened the day for the people who waited on her and left them with smiles on their faces. She had a huge appetite for life and for food.

Lizzie's first errand of the day was going to the bank. Her father, Bob, would use the drive-up window, so that Lizzie could interact with the bank's drive-up teller. After Bob did the family's banking business, the teller would talk to Lizzie, compliment her on her latest coat or sweater, and give her dog biscuits for herself and her four other pack members: Chewy, a white and brown Siberian Husky-German Shepherd mix with light blue eyes, Gilligana, a black Labrador retriever mix, Daisy, a large buff cocker spaniel, and Maverick, a white and reddish-brown Jack Russell Terrier-Beagle mix.

From the bank, Lizzie and her family went on to the local McDonald's restaurant drive-up window for breakfast, where she and her pack members would each get a piece of egg or sausage from their parents' Miranda's and Bob's egg, sausage, and muffin sandwiches.

After breakfast, Lizzie and her family went to the Fast Friends Dog Park. At the gate, they were greeted by Lizzie's pal, Edwin, a rescued pit bull terrier. They sniffed noses and play-bowed. Then Edwin chased Lizzie all around the dog park's fenced-in area while her pack members all joined in ball and Frisbee games with the other dogs. After twenty minutes of playing, everyone's tongues were hanging out and they were panting hard. Their parents gave them each some water and decided to go to Lizzie's favorite dog bakery next.

At the I Want a Biscuit Dog Bakery, Lizzie marched up to the counter and started barking to announce that she was there. A kindly old man came out from the back room and gave Lizzie some warm samples of carob-carrot, barbecue, cinnamon-apple, and peanut butter shortbread biscuits. Her favorite was the peanut butter shortbread biscuit, so she selected that kind for herself and one of each of the other types for her four pack members. As she was leaving, Lizzie saw and greeted her pal, Sunny, coming in the door.

Sunny was a rescued greyhound that went to the bakery every Saturday at 10 AM. They had become very good friends. Before they left the bakery building, Lizzie and her pals went into a private room where Rebecca, an animal communicator (a dog psychic), was waiting for them. She was there to tell Miranda and Bob what their dogs were thinking and saying to them. Before they even started, Rebecca said that one dog was coming through very strongly. Of course, that dog turned out to be Lizzie. She wanted to know if she was going to get more cookies.

Rebecca then brought up things that each dog wanted to know or tell Bob and Miranda. They included requests for special foods and toys, their likes or dislikes for certain pack members, and health issues. When the reading was finished, they all walked outside of the room, where other people and their dogs were waiting in a line. Lizzie started barking at one of the dogs in the line, so Bob hustled her and the other pack members out of the building fast.

After the dogs' reading with Rebecca, then it was on to the Pinecone Travel Plaza Truck Stop for water and bathroom breaks. Their father, Bob, pulled up to gas pump #1, which her parents called "Lizzie's Pump," and filled up the gas tank. Bob paid for the gas and pulled the car off to the side near a grassy area. The parents walked the dogs, so that they could go to the bathroom and drink some water. Nearby, Bob took a picture of Miranda and Lizzie standing in front of a large pink elephant statue wearing black eye glasses. Then they all left to go to one of Lizzie's favorite stores, Pet Smart.

Bob took Lizzie into Pet Smart, while Miranda stayed with the rest of the dogs in the car with all of the windows rolled down. Lizzie barked to announce herself as she entered the store and some people came up to her and petted her, saying how cute she was in her hooded sweater outfit. Lizzie selected rawhide chews, domestically-made beef jerky treats, and a new collar with a matching leash for herself. At the cash register, Bob paid for the items. On their way out of the store, Lizzie growled at a larger dog. Bob scolded her and hustled her out quickly to her waiting family in the car.

From Pet Smart, Lizzie and her parents took her four larger siblings to the Fun Times Dog Motel for an overnight stay. The four dogs left with the attendants to go back to their kennels. They had been to the hotel before and liked the scheduled walks and supervised playtimes that they got during their stays there.

Then Lizzie went with her parents to an outdoor drive-in movie. As the car approached the ticket office, her parents hid her under a blanket. Lizzie barked once and threw the blanket off of her head. The ticket seller looked down into the car at Lizzie, smiled, and waved the car through the gates. After it got dark, the three of them watched "Air Spud," a movie about a dog who grew up on a potato farm and became a great basketball player.

During the intermission, Liz's parents went to use the rest rooms, which were very close to their car. When Miranda and Bob returned to the car, they found Lizzie gobbling up the remains of an entire submarine sandwich that Bob had stuffed under his car seat. Obviously, he had not hidden it well enough!

After the movie ended, Lizzie and her parents went to a motel that allows small dogs to stay there with their humans. As Lizzie and her parents approached the motel clerk's desk, she barked to announce herself. After they all checked in, they went up to their motel room, where they watched TV, ate treats, and retired for the night.

Conclusion

Lizzie died three years ago, but her memory lives on for her parents, Bob and Miranda, in the little things that get done each day, such as errands. On Saturdays, their current errand dogs: Spud, Ashley May, and Buster go on errands with them that Lizzie used to do. Not only are the errands more fun with their dogs, but Miranda and Bob fondly remember Lizzie at each of the locations that she used to visit.

THE BEAGLE BOYS: MAVERICK AND SPEEDY ARE FRIENDS

Introduction to Maverick

Maverick was a very muscular two-year-old reddish-brown and white beagle-Jack Russell terrier mix. When we got Maverick as a foster dog who had come up to a Wisconsin rescue from Missouri, he had heartworm disease and had to go through painful shots. He had to stay at the veterinary clinic for one day for observation. When Bob went to the clinic to bring Maverick home, he heard him barking very loudly over all of the other dogs. It was obvious that he wanted to go back to his home. There, Maverick had to be kept quiet and prevented from engaging in the vigorous play and exercise that he loved. After his recovery from heartworms, he was neutered.

Miranda and Bob never intended to adopt Maverick, but they slowly fell in love with him. He was an active dog who loved being a dog and doing doggie things. He liked to play, eat, and go for walks with their other dogs and fit right in with their entire family.

"Mavie," as they called him, had them--his father, Bob, and his mother, Miranda, on a schedule everyday—Bob would walk him with one of their other dogs, Daisy, a large buff cocker Spaniel mix, every morning and evening. Miranda would give them their food, vitamins, and treats, and daily teeth-brushing and grooming.

Miranda and Bob decided to adopt Maverick, because they liked how well he fit in with their three cocker spaniels—Lizzie (small and buff-colored), Spud (small and white, black, and brown), and Daisy (large and buff-colored) and because they did not want Maverick to feel that they did not want him; nor did they want Maverick to be torn from a family that he had come to love and have to start all over once again. In addition to all of this, Bob and Miranda felt that going through those difficult experiences along with Maverick bonded them to him even more.

Newly-Adopted Maverick

Because Maverick was bright and active, he soon became bored with his different toys. He even destroyed one of their television remotes. He enjoyed pulling the stuffing out of all of his stuffed toys, pillows, and quilted blankets and figured out how to get the treats out of his Kong treat dispensers. Maverick did not want to play ball anymore, and when Miranda and Bob tried to get Spud, their six-year-old white, black, and brown cocker spaniel to play with him, Spud was not interested in puppy play at all.

Introduction to Rugaard

Bob and Miranda were starting to get worried about how bored and depressed Maverick seemed to be getting, so they decided to go to a shelter and get a playmate for Maverick. They saw a very small and friendly dog named Rugaard. He was a two-year-old brown beagle with short stubby white bowed legs and a long brown, white, and black tail. Rugaard looked like he was smiling and was wagging his tail at them from his enclosure. One of the shelter volunteers was taking Rugaard out of his enclosure to go outside and play with Rascal, a dog who was in the enclosure next to him. Rascal was a black and brown collie mix who was playing very roughly with Rugaard and landing on top of him repeatedly with all of his weight.

Miranda was worried about Rascal being too rough with the much smaller Rugaard as they watched them go out to the shelter's play yard together to play. Bob and Miranda continued to walk past the enclosures of the other dogs in the shelter, but they both liked Rugaard and kept coming back to his enclosure. After he returned from the play yard with Rascal, other people started pouring in to view the dogs. Two old ladies slowly walked past the cages and they both were worried that these other people were going to take a shine to Rugaard. They passed his enclosure without stopping, but Miranda and Bob decided that they were not going to take any chances and went to find a shelter attendant. They found a lady named Susan and they asked her to let them meet Rugaard in the introduction room. Susan said that she had given this dog the name Rugaard, because it was the name of a beloved dragon character in book 3, "Dragon Outcast," a novel from her favorite fantasy/adventure series: "Age of Fire" by E. E. Knight.

Miranda's and Bob's Dogs Meet Rugaard

Bob and Miranda told Susan, the shelter volunteer, that they were concerned about how Rugaard would get along with their four other dogs—Maverick, Lizzie, Spud, and Daisy, who were waiting in the car with the windows opened in the cold April air. They also told her that they wanted a playmate for Maverick, so they brought Maverick in first to meet Rugaard. They sniffed each other and Rugaard went belly-up on his back. After this short introduction, Rugaard stood up and Maverick chased him around the room until Rugaard jumped up on a table.

After some time elapsed, it was time for Rugaard to meet their three other dogs. Their three cocker spaniels, Daisy, Spud, and Lizzie, walked around the meet and greet room while Maverick and Rugaard were playing with a toy that was on the floor. Everyone got along, so Miranda and Bob went ahead and adopted Rugaard, who rode home with all of them in their car. Rugaard would never see Rascal again.

Rugaard Becomes Speedy Rugrat

After knowing Rugaard for a few days, Bob and Miranda realized that he was very smart. They decided to re-name him Speedy, because he was speedy both mentally and physically and because they had trouble remembering the name Rugaard. They almost named him Einstein, because he rang a bell that was hung around the knob of our front door on his first day with them. This was something that none of their other dogs had done. Miranda and Bob also decided to give Speedy the middle name of Rugrat, which seemed similar to Rugaard and which was a name that they could remember better.

Speedy, Formerly Rugaard

Maverick and Speedy bonded as playmates immediately and they would play for hours with each other. When the two dogs would play, sometimes they would snarl and bare their teeth at each other. Then Bob and Miranda would call an end to their play session and separate them before it erupted into a fight. There have been times when they would get into a fight and Miranda and Bob would separate them and yell at them to stop it.

Maverick and Speedy never held grudges with each other and became best friends. They did everything together—they walked on trails with their other pack members in their backyard dog park, napped with each other, played with each other, walked on the treadmill side-by-side, and even howled together during their daily sing-alongs led by Miranda.

Maverick and Speedy Enjoying the Fire

When Maverick and Speedy played, sometimes they'd get up on their hind legs with their front legs on each other's necks; other times, they'd each bite the same toy animal, shake it, and try to pull it apart in a tug of war. Maverick and Speedy loved to tear the stuffing out of their toys and pillows. Miranda and Bob finally learned to provide the two playmates with plush, long toys that looked like foxes, skunks, snakes, and other animals but did not have stuffing in them. They also provided beds without pillows.

Maverick and Speedy had still another favorite activity, where they enjoyed pulling three little stuffed squeaky squirrels out of a stuffed log with holes. Eventually they got two more plush toys like the squirrel log—they were a beehive with squeaky bees and a bird house with squeaky birds.

As Maverick and Speedy have grown up, they don't play much with each other in the house anymore, but they do chase and play with each other outside on the trails of their backyard dog park.

Conclusion

Wherever Miranda and Bob took Speedy, people would laugh and smile at him. They thought that it was because he had short legs and his body was close to the ground. Speedy still looked like a puppy, even though he was an adult. The veterinary technician at their clinic said that Speedy was the cutest beagle that she had ever seen. Speedy liked to surprise people and lick their faces, too, which made him even more endearing!

Bob and Miranda recently had a DNA test performed on Speedy and the test results determined that Speedy was part beagle and part Yorkshire terrier. Perhaps the Yorkshire terrier genetics are what kept Speedy small.

In any event, Speedy was a cute little dog and he provided Maverick, their other dogs, and Miranda and Bob with hours of play, laughter, and companionship. They are very grateful that Speedy turned out to be a very good choice of a friend and playmate for Maverick. Bob and Miranda followed up with the animal shelter where they had adopted Speedy to see what happened to Rascal and were happy to hear that he had been adopted. They hoped that Rascal had found a playmate that was as good as Speedy!

I CALLED SPUD CHEWY

Introduction to Chewy

Experiencing the sicknesses and deaths of our pets is probably the hardest part of pet ownership. Just like humans, every animal will eventually die, and it is very likely that our dogs will die before us, because their lives are so short compared to ours. A human being can live up to 100 or more years; whereas, dogs live an average of twelve to fifteen years, with the larger dogs dying sooner and the smaller dogs dying later.

Chewy was a beautiful Siberian husky and German shepherd mix. His head was that of a white husky with beautiful, ice-blue eyes and his body was that of a brown and black German shepherd with white paws and a pink nose.

Miranda and Bob met Chewy, whose shelter name was Ranger, as a four-month-old puppy at their area humane society. Chewy was in the first kennel and would greet people like a receptionist with a broad smile and fast-wagging tail. As they opened the door and entered the kennel room, they saw Chewy and fell in love with his friendliness. After looking at all of the other dogs, Bob and Miranda decided to adopt Chewy. They were told by the adoption counselor that Chewy had only been there at the shelter for fifteen minutes.

Miranda and Bob felt lucky to have found Chewy and felt that he would not have been at the shelter for another fifteen minutes, as certainly someone certainly would have adopted him—he was that cute! They felt that their timing on that day was just right and that they were meant to have Chewy in their family. Bob and Miranda waited for Chewy to be micro-chipped and then they took him home.

Chewy's Life with Miranda and Bob

Chewy was a very cute puppy, but he grew up quite fast. One of Bob's and Miranda's earlier memories of Chewy was that he got into a fight over food with their other dog, Gilligana, a Halden hound. When Miranda heard Chewy crying, she came into the room and found Chewy's ear torn and his nose bleeding. Miranda took Chewy into the bath tub, stopped the bleeding, and wrapped his wounds.

A second memory that Miranda and Bob have of Chewy was that they couldn't walk him out much in public, because he would start barking and lunging at other dogs on the parkway. They suspected that he might have been attacked by a dog as a puppy and was afraid that all dogs attacked. After several of these incidents, Bob and Miranda reduced the frequency of Chewy's walks and he became more of an indoor or house dog. Inside their house, Chewy enjoyed being a watch dog and would bark and howl like a wolf whenever people came to their door.

A third memory that Miranda and Bob had of Chewy was that even though he was neutered, they found that Chewy was marking or spraying books and other items in their house. One of the books was a travel book on their state's waterfalls and Miranda was not happy to find it all wet and wrinkled; still she refused to part with the book and hung it up over the shower curtain rod to dry out.

Bob's and Miranda's fourth and most vivid memory of Chewy involved their being up at their vacation cottage. They had just built their cottage and brought their dogs to stay at it for the first time. Chewy, Gilligana, Lizzie, and Miranda had all gone into the cottage when they heard dogs barking. Miranda and Chewy looked out of the side bedroom window and there were two Doberman pinschers barking quite vigorously at them right through their window. Chewy then barked back at them and they eventually retreated, or so they thought.

Miranda and Chewy then went to the front of the cottage and looked out of the windows to see Bob on top of their car with the two dogs barking at him. Bob just looked at the two seemingly vicious dogs while Chewy kept barking at them. After five or ten minutes, the two dogs finally left. This was their "welcome" to the neighborhood. After this incident, they nicknamed these two dogs, "Mutt and Jeff." Although Miranda and Bob talked about Mutt and Jeff for months after the incident, they never saw them again and never found out where they lived. They were just glad that Chewy was there to stand up to these two dogs. He didn't seem afraid of them at all; of course, it helped that he was safe inside the house when he did it.

Bob's and Miranda's fifth memory of Chewy that stands out also involved his protectiveness during another incident that happened at their cottage. Chewy and Miranda were staying up at the cottage alone for a few days with no car parked in their driveway.

One day, a young man came walking up the driveway with a black husky. As soon as Chewy saw the pair, he started barking at them through the window. The young man then turned around and they walked back down the driveway and onto the road. The area of their property where the man was headed smelled like it had been visited by dogs a lot. After this incident, they knew who had been walking his dog there on a regular basis. They surmised that this young man had thought that no one was home because there was no car in the driveway, so he could walk his dog on their property. Here, Chewy had come through for them again!

Chewy's Death

Chewy always tried his best to protect Miranda's and Bob's family and it was very hard to find out that they couldn't do much to protect him. One day, Chewy had a seizure. To them, it looked like he was rotating around and around on the floor and could not get up.

Bob took Chewy to their vet and he was diagnosed with lymphoma, a cancer of the lymph glands, and was told that it was possibly spreading to his brain. With Miranda's father's very generous financial gift, they were able to treat Chewy with chemotherapy, which prolonged his life for seven months. He lived from August through March.

Just like with human chemotherapy patients, Chewy's hair started to fall out. It wasn't noticeable on Chewy, though, because he had a thick, double coat of fur. The veterinary technicians at the vet's office all loved seeing Chewy and knew him by name. He didn't seem to mind those visits. In fact, Bob and Miranda thought that Chewy enjoyed all of the attention that he was getting, even though he was sick and getting treatments that were rough on his body.

One day, when Chewy was napping, Miranda and Bob noticed that he became unconscious, unresponsive, and cold to the touch. Bob took him to the Emergency Vet Center, where he was pronounced dead on arrival.

Chewy Napping

Chewy was cremated, and his ashes were put into a beautiful wooden box with a frame holding his picture. They also received a clay paw print of Chewy's paw from the cremation service.

Mementoes of Chewy

It was very hard for Bob, Miranda, and their dogs to say goodbye to Chewy after twelve wonderful years of knowing and loving him. They were comforted, though, by the fact that they made every effort to spoil Chewy in his last days. During the extra seven months that they got to have with Chewy, they showered him with the two things that he loved most—walks and meat. Every night, Bob took Chewy out for walks and every day, Miranda gave Chewy meat from her meals.

Looking back, Miranda wished that she had kept more of Chewy's hair tufts that she found all over the house instead of throwing them away. She put what hair she had of his inside a pillow with his photo on it. Also, now Miranda treasures the wrinkled book that Chewy peed on. It's funny how time changes how we think and feel about events— Miranda and Bob treasure all of the memories and physical mementos that they have left of Chewy.

After Chewy's death, Bob and Miranda got Spud, a tri parti (three-colored) cocker spaniel--black and white, with a small amount of brown coloring on his face. Miranda had always envisioned getting a dog named Spud—only he was going to be a large black-faced German Shepherd—not a small black and white cocker spaniel. She was surprised when her wish for having a dog named Spud came true.

Their New Dog, Spud

Spud never met Chewy, but Miranda made sure that she told Spud all about Chewy over the next few months. She noticed that Spud would sometimes lie down right in the same place at the top of their stairs and peer down at them from where Chewy did the exact same thing.

Miranda even caught herself calling Spud "Chewy" a few times. She was sure, though, that Spud didn't mind. Perhaps Spud instinctively knew that Miranda would be telling another young pup stories about him someday.

Conclusion

The lesson here is that in pet ownership, just like in life, we have to take the bad with the good. The time when our animal is young is a fun-filled and easy time of his/her life. As our pets get older, they start to slow down, develop diseases, and die.

Grief is a pretty certain part of pet ownership, because most of the time, our dogs die before we do. Most dog parents feel guilty about euthanizing their old or sick dogs, but sometimes it is a very loving gesture if a dog is suffering greatly and has no quality of life anymore. We have to make sure that our pets feel loved while we have them, because it is certain that one day they will be gone.

It is a privilege to have dogs, and it is our duty to see to it that they have great lives, and as much as possible, comfortable deaths.

ASHLEY, THE BLACK DOG

Introduction to Ashley

Ashley was a smaller-than-average black cocker spaniel who came to Miranda and Bob from a high-kill shelter in Kentucky. When they adopted Ashley they were told by her rescue agency that a dog like her would have been put to sleep. Bob and Miranda asked why and were told that she would go blind due to cataracts, had cherry eye, and was a black dog, and that for those reasons, no one would want her.

Ashley, Sitting Pretty

To delve further for an explanation, Miranda and Bob asked why her black coloring was a problem for people. They were told that just like in human history, where some people have been prejudiced against black people due to the color of their skin, some people seem to have a prejudice against black dogs because of the color of their fur. Bob and Miranda were flabbergasted! They wondered how could this be true?

Their Ashley was a very sweet and loving dog, and they loved her very much. She was very fearful in the beginning—especially with Bob—and would not come to either of them when they called her. Despite her shyness, Ashley never missed a meal time and she got along very well with her other five pack members.

Miranda and Bob had four male dogs and each one liked Ashley. She was not spayed when they adopted her, as they figured that she had probably been used for breeding purposes in a puppy mill. There were times that Miranda would catch Maverick, our Jack Russell and Beagle mix, mating with Ashley. They would wait until she left them alone in the room and she would discover them joined together when she came back.

Bob's and Miranda's other three dogs liked Ashley too. Wherever Spud, their white, black, and brown tri-colored cocker spaniel went, Ashley went too. Speedy, their little beagle mix, would come up to Ashley and lick the tears from her eyes and face. At different times, Ashley would play bow, charge, and invite Maverick, Buster, and Spud to chase her. Their larger-than-normal cocker spaniel, Daisy, ignored Ashley, but then Daisy ignored everyone but Bob.

Spud and Ashley, Two Good Pals

Whether it was day or night, Ashley liked to go under the bed to sleep. Miranda and Bob thought that it was like a den for her, where she could feel safe. Miranda couldn't help but think that maybe she hid somewhere when she had her puppies. She noticed that Ashley liked taking all of the rawhide chews out of the dogs' toy box, chewing on one or two, and then leaving the rest out on the rug for Miranda to pick up later.

Because Ashley was so pretty and feminine and had a shiny coat, Miranda bought her a pink rhinestone-studded collar and a wardrobe consisting of three different sundresses.

She was tempted to put barrettes on her ears, but an animal communicator told them during a reading that a previous female owner had done that and that Ashley did not like it. The communicator urged Miranda to abandon that idea for Ashley's sake and she was happy to do so.

Ashley with Her Pink Rhinestone Collar

When Bob and Miranda first adopted Ashley, she had three medical problems that really concerned them: 1) her cataracts; 2) her urinary tract infection; and 3) her tendency to gain weight easily.

Miranda and Bob were very pleased to treat Ashley's eyes with drops that are called Nu-Eyes TM distributed by Bio National Pharmaceuticals, a company in California. Miranda did some research and found out about these eye drops through the internet. She learned that humans had used the eye drops and they were reporting that they were seeing things better than they had before. This testing done previously on humans was an advantage, because Ashley wouldn't be able to tell them if she was seeing things better. Miranda thought that these drops stopped the cataracts from enlarging, and they were happy to announce that Ashley saw things well and did not go blind as was previously predicted for her by her rescue organization.

Ashley's second problem, the urinary tract infection, went away with antibiotic pills, but she still kept urinating on Bob's and Miranda's rugs three-to-five times per day. For awhile they tried to avoid the accidents by letting Ashley out every hour, but this got tiresome and hard to keep doing.

Ashley's third problem was her ability to gain weight easily. She loved to eat and was always there at meal times. Miranda and Bob found that after they fenced in their backyard, Ashley was running around and getting much more exercise than before. They still had to watch Ashley's weight, but the increased exercise made her a much happier and healthier dog. Miranda believed that other people would have adopted Ashley and treated her medical issues if her fur had been a different color.

Bob and Miranda finally found a solution to Ashley's incontinence problem-- using pants that had a hole in them for the tail and that were made for females when they are in heat. They got the idea when they needed belly bands, a type of pants made for male dogs, designed to keep them from marking inside homes. This use of pants on Ashley was very effective and she no longer had any accidents inside their home. Miranda guessed that living with so many male dogs had had an influence on Ashley, because when she walked outside with them, Miranda noticed that Ashley was lifting her leg to urinate like male dogs do. Miranda was intrigued, because she had never seen a female dog do that.

Ashley's Cute Purple Pants

Miranda and Bob were very relieved that two simple products like eye drops and dog pants solved two problems that at one time seemed unsolvable for them.

It was hard for Bob and Miranda to believe that someone wouldn't want a dog, because she or he has black fur, but this practice has been documented and discussed in online newsletters and on television. Miranda was told that people in the animal rescue field are very familiar with this phenomenon and that it is called "black dog syndrome."

Dr. Karen Becker discussed the reasons why people are afraid of adopting black dogs and the things that animal shelters can do to eliminate the overlooking of black dogs by potential adoptive parents in her article entitled, "Pet Adoption: Will These Pets Ever Find Homes?" This article was posted by Dr. Becker on February 1, 2012 and can be found on the healthypets.mercola.com website.

In her article, Dr. Becker mentioned such reasons for not selecting black dogs as: superstitious beliefs, black dogs looking older than other dogs, harder-to-see facial expressions on black dogs, and black hair left on furniture. She also cited things that shelters can do to overcome black dog syndrome, such as: alternating black dogs so that they are not all in a row, using eye-catching colorful toys, scarves, and blankets to draw attention to black dogs, well-lit photography, and half-price adoption events on all black animals.

Conclusion

Miranda and Bob felt that people should welcome adopting black pets, because if they had let black dog syndrome prejudice them, they would have missed out on a wonderful little dog. Ashley followed Miranda around wherever she went. She was a loyal companion, a great pack member, a great trail walker, and one of Miranda's closest friends! Since they added Ashley, Bob and Miranda now have 3 black dogs and one black cat and would not hesitate to add more black animals to their pack.

Reference

Becker, Dr. Karen. "Will These Pets Ever Find Homes?" Retrieved February 1, 2012, from http://healthypets.mercola.com/sites/healthypets/archive/2012/02/01/wil...

BUSTER, THE LOVEABLE CURMUDGEON

Introduction to Buster

This is a story about Buster, who growled all or most of the time; yet, he was basically a loveable, funny, and non-aggressive good sport who became a part of Miranda's and Bob's pack. When you think about a growling dog with his teeth bared, it generally means that that dog is angry about something and wants you to stop or back away. It is usually one of the warning signs that a dog is about to become aggressive. This was not the case with Buster, who was like a paper tiger—all growl and no bite.

Bob and Miranda first heard about Buster in an e-mail from an older lady who couldn't take care of him anymore and was giving him up. She was looking for someone to adopt or rescue Buster and her daughter posted the notice online in an animal transport group members' forum.

When Miranda read the posting about Buster, she thought that he would just sit in a rescue facility and that no one would want to adopt him, as he was a whitish-gray Shih Tzu who growled and marked. Miranda answered the lady's daughter, telling her that Bob and she already had dogs who both growled and marked in their pack and that they were quite used to it.

Their large honey-colored cocker spaniel, Daisy, growled all of the time, but she never bit anyone and was a very loyal companion to Bob. Maverick, their beagle-Jack Russell Terrier mix, was a night-time bed-wetter and daytime indoor marker, and Speedy their cute beagle mix, was an avid indoor marker. Both of these dogs had to wear belly bands when they were in the house.

After communicating back-and-forth through e-mails with the lady's daughter and a home visit, Miranda and Bob were able to adopt Buster. Every few months, Miranda would send the lady's daughter updates of Buster's progress along with his photos to forward to her mother, who still had Buster's sister, Princess.

Buster's Ride Home

Buster's Growling

When Bob and Miranda got Buster, they noticed that he growled at everything and everyone—if they petted him, played with him, picked him up or moved him, covered him with a blanket, bathed him, clipped his fur, dressed him, etc. After several months of trying to get Buster to stop growling, they stopped and just accepted it as part of his engrained personality.

When Miranda and Bob would introduce new dogs to their pack, they were worried that Buster's incessant growling would antagonize their new dogs into fighting with him, but thankfully, their dogs learned to ignore his growling and regard him as a noise-maker or boy who was crying wolf. Buster was assertive and growled at or followed their other dogs to scold them if they got too close, bumped into him, or stepped on him by mistake.

Buster's Marking

Because Bob and Miranda had other dogs with incontinence and marking problems, they were already familiar with using belly bands on two of their male dogs, Maverick and Speedy. Like Maverick and Speedy, Buster loved marking both indoors and outdoors. When Buster was outside, he would watch and wait for their other dogs to mark; then he would mark over the spot where they just marked. As a result, Miranda and Bob used belly bands on Buster in the house, and it was no longer a problem.

Buster's Coprophagia

Miranda noticed that Buster had a habit of eating dog stool, so she was concerned about him getting sick and having terrible breath. Miranda read that this waste-eating is due to a dog's lacking stomach enzymes for digesting his food. Miranda ordered the coprophagia deterrence pills that treat that condition, but she didn't want to make their other dogs eat them when it was really Buster's problem. Instead, Miranda tied Buster to a lead when he went out to relieve himself. She would watch him and if she saw him starting to eat his own stool, she would pull on the lead and that would make him come running into the house. Since Miranda started using the lead method, Buster does not eat dog waste anymore. She is very happy that he does not do this practice anymore!

Buster's Special Diet

Buster came to Bob and Miranda with a mouth of rotten teeth, foul-smelling breath, and a heart murmur. Buster had to have all of his teeth pulled, which resulted in a $600 dental bill. After his teeth were pulled, Buster's bad breath went away. Miranda would prepare a bowl of soft food for Buster, who was not able to eat the dry, hard dog food that they fed to their dogs that still had their teeth. At first, he wouldn't eat anything that Miranda offered him, and she was getting worried.

Then Miranda discovered that Buster liked wieners, and later, she added chicken pieces to the wieners and he ate that too. After Miranda and Bob adopted their dachshund, Rusty, who was also toothless except for one tooth, Miranda started making a mixture of hamburger and vegetables from a recipe given to them by Rusty's foster mother. Miranda started adding this meat and vegetable mixture to Buster's food bowl and he ate it.

The last thing that Miranda added to Buster's bowl was a series of vitamins—an herbal multi-vitamin powder for dogs and cats, vitamin C powder for his immunity, glucosamine chondroitin powder to protect his brittle joints, and fish oil for his skin and coat.

Over the months since they adopted Buster, the color of his fur coat changed from a dry whitish-gray to a luxurious and shiny, black. Miranda thought that this miraculous change was due to these vitamins—especially the fish oil. Also, Buster had boundless energy and he was always the last dog to want to come in from their pack's walks on their backyard trails.

Buster's Thunder Phobia

Bob and Miranda never had a dog who had thunder phobia before. It was hard for them to watch Buster have panic attacks anytime that there was a thunderstorm—day or night! He would start pacing back and forth, trembling, and salivating. Before anything else, they would put Buster in his thunder shirt to calm him down. If they put him in his crate, he would keep clawing at the door trying to get out of it. Miranda gave Buster tranquility tablets, used a few drops of Bach's herbal remedy on his blanket, and sprayed a puppy pheromone near him to calm him down until the storm was over.

They guessed that in his earlier years in the puppy mill, Buster may have been kept in a cage outdoors and had nowhere to hide when storms came. They imagined how frightening and terrifying it must have been for him to be outside during these storms.

Bob always had a hard time taking pictures of Buster, because he would run away and hide. Miranda figured that Buster didn't like having his pictures taken, because the camera flashes reminded him of lightning. To this day, Buster still turns away from the camera, as he does in this photo of himself modeling his thunder shirt.

Buster in His Thunder Shirt

Buster's Breakthroughs with Rusty, Ashley, Spud, and the Choir

After Miranda and Bob had Buster for seven months, they adopted another mill dog, Rusty, who was a smooth-haired red dachshund. Rusty was in a lot of pain when he came home with them from his foster parents' home. He had just had all but one of his teeth removed and the dental infection had started to eat its way through his nose to his face; he also had been neutered.

Rusty Sleeping After His Operations

As Rusty lay on their bed groaning, Buster came up to him and acted like he was guarding Rusty. For Bob and Miranda, it was an unexpected, but very welcome, surprise—they didn't know that Buster was capable of feeling such love, compassion, and protectiveness for anyone. Previously Buster had acted like the "tough guy" who doesn't want to be friends with anyone, including Miranda and Bob. Miranda thought that perhaps Buster felt this way toward Rusty, because Buster had already gone through the same medical procedures with his teeth and neutering.

Buster by Rusty's Side

Another welcome event with Buster took one year in the making. When Buster first came to Bob and Miranda, Ashley, their small black cocker spaniel, would repeatedly play bow to Buster, inviting him to be playful with her. For about one year, Buster ignored Ashley's overtures. Then one day, Buster surprised Miranda by play bowing to Ashley, jumping up on her while standing on his hind legs, and chasing her all over the house. Miranda and Bob had been told that Buster used to play with his sister, Princess, but they never saw any evidence of it until that time. The tides turned, and Ashley would actually hide from Buster when she got tired from playing with and being chased by Buster.

A third breakthrough happened for Buster when he and Spud were returning home from the veterinary clinic where they had had their booster vaccinations. Usually Buster would stay far away from the other dogs in his pack, but both he and Spud slept cuddled together in the front seat with Bob on the way home. Bob and Miranda had never seen Buster welcome physical contact from anyone before—usually he would growl if anyone touched him.

Buster Cuddling With Spud after their Vet Visit

Finally, Miranda and Bob were very surprised one day to see that Buster had joined Miranda during her sing-alongs or more appropriately called howl-alongs with their two beagle mixes, Maverick and Speedy, and their dachshund, Rusty. Buster's howling was at a higher pitch and sounded a little raspy. It was hard to hear Buster, because he would be drowned out by the other three singing hounds and other dogs of theirs who would join in by barking; yet Miranda could tell that Buster was singing if his head was pointed up toward the ceiling with his mouth wide open. Buster seemed very into the moment or passionate when he was singing. Miranda thought that either Buster enjoyed it or that it was another way for Buster to feel like he was a part of their pack!

Conclusion

These touching and surprising events with Buster have shown Bob and Miranda that even though he had a tough exterior, there were soft and fun sides to his personality as well. Because Buster was a tiny, eight-pound dog, Miranda guessed that he probably was over-compensating to protect himself. He walked around their house with his blanket dragging behind him like a little prince with a train. Also, when Buster was on a mission, such as going outside for a walk or coming for dinner, he walked with a very confident spring in his step. It seemed that his large personality was not dwarfed by his small size.

Little Prince Buster

Every animal has some good qualities, even if they seem like they don't. Those good qualities just have to be brought out by the right humans, animals, and situations. Miranda and Bob learned that it's not always possible or even important to try to change your animal's behavior. Sometimes it is an integral, endearing, or comical part of an animal's personality and it's best to let your animals just be who they are.

BUTTERSCOTCH AND GATSBY, STRANGE BEDFELLOWS

Introduction to Butterscotch

Miranda first heard about a very friendly and outgoing stray yellow cat through a state online transport group. One of the group's members, Jennifer, had posted information that she was feeding a cat that ran up to her near her garage in April. He had frostbitten ears and she was letting him stay in her garage. Jennifer mentioned that she wanted this cat to have a home and be able to live indoors as part of a family. She also stated in her e-mail that she already had four cats and two dogs and that her husband would not let her have any more cats.

Butterscotch, the Friendly Cat

Miranda sent Jennifer an e-mail saying that Bob and she were dog-lovers and that they did not know anything about having cats, but that they would like to adopt this one and give him a home. Miranda recalled to Jennifer an incident with a farm cat that had happened to her in her childhood and that that event had kept her from considering adopting cats for many decades. Miranda told her that she knew that there were millions of cat owners in our country, though, and that she wanted to see what it was that made so many people love their cats.

The incident happened at Miranda's grandparents' house on a farm, where she was vacationing one summer. Miranda was standing on a driveway that led to the barns and was welcomed by a very large, yellow tom cat. She bent down and squatted to pet the friendly cat. Miranda thought nothing of it when he walked behind her. He then climbed up on Miranda's back and stuck his claws into her back. At that point, Miranda stood up, causing the cat to fall off of her back and run away. After that incident, she carried the idea with her that all cats were like that feral barn cat and would claw her if given the chance. Miranda told Jennifer that this sweet cat could be good for her, and that she was ready for him to show her that all cats are not like that.

Butterscotch's Arrival

Miranda arranged with Jennifer for Jennifer to bring the stray yellow cat to their cottage. After she arrived, she brought him inside in a crate and let him out in Miranda's and Bob's living room. The cat walked all around the house, exploring every room that was open to him. He sniffed around closets and under the refrigerator—all places where mice had been found in the past. He also went under the bed and had to be coaxed to come out.

So that the cat could freely explore the house in peace and quiet, Miranda had secluded some of their dogs in the bathroom with the door closed and Bob had taken the remaining dogs to the carpeted and heated garage to play.

Miranda showed Jennifer the small bedroom with file cabinets and a closet which they used as a file room, as this was going to be the cat's room. Jennifer asked Miranda if she knew what she wanted to name the friendly cat and she said, "Butterscotch," because he was sweet, smooth, and mellow like butterscotch candy. In the sun, Butterscotch looked more beige, while in darker light, he looked more orange. From doing some online searching, Miranda concluded that he would be called a red tabby by cat experts.

While at Bob's and Miranda's house, Jennifer gave Miranda some toys for Butterscotch—a little tinsel ball, a long strip of animal print polar fleece, and a small shocking pink mouse. She also left Butterscotch a round, two-level toy that contained balls inside it. Butterscotch must have played with this toy before, because he readily moved the balls around inside of it with his paw.

Besides the toys, Jennifer had brought a large litter box and scoop and recommended that Miranda and Bob use clumping litter rather than plain clay litter. She also showed Miranda what the waste products looked like after Butterscotch used the litter box. In addition, she left with Miranda some cat food and a tube of a salmon-flavored gel that should be given to Butterscotch regularly to fight the formation of fur balls and aid in their elimination. Then she gave Miranda a soft, flat cat bed and a book about cats. The only things that they still needed to get were cat food and water dishes, cat treats, and a cat tree.

Before Jennifer left Miranda's and Bob's house, she said that she would be glad to answer any questions that came up and would be glad to visit Butterscotch whenever she was doing animal transports in their area again.

After Jennifer left, Butterscotch went to the bathroom behind the fire stove, jumped up on the top of the couch, and then jumped down onto a credenza, knocking a picture frame to the floor. The picture frame glass was not broken, so luckily, Butterscotch was not hurt. After this incident, Bob and Miranda decided that it would be best if Butterscotch stayed in his own room where he could climb, jump, and run to his heart's content without getting hurt. Also, they would not have to worry about Butterscotch escaping out through the back door while the dogs were going out or out through the front door if they were receiving visitors.

Getting to Know Butterscotch

Because Bob was still in the process of moving things up to their cottage, there was a bottom file cabinet in Butterscotch's room that did not have a drawer in it yet. In his first week or two with them, Butterscotch would lie in the space on the floor where the file cabinet drawer was supposed to be. A week later, Bob brought the file cabinet drawer and Butterscotch lost his hiding and sleeping space; it seemed, though, that Butterscotch was feeling more comfortable and safe living with Miranda and Bob, and he no longer felt the need to hide when he slept at night.

50

Bob bought a carpeted cat tree for Butterscotch, with two roped scratching posts, a cube, and two perches, but Butterscotch would not use it much—it was Gatsby who would later become its primary user.

At Miranda's request, Bob built a cat perch, which amounted to a wooden shelf mounted and braced at the window, where Butterscotch could watch the parade of wildlife who visited daily. There were birds at the feeders and chipmunks and squirrels were running around and in the many wood piles that they had on that side of their house.

Whenever Miranda entered the room, Butterscotch would always run to her and rub against her legs. Then Miranda would brush him with a brush and he would purr continuously. Butterscotch especially liked the brush on his face and would actively rub his cheeks and chin against the bristles of the brush. Then Miranda would put down the brush and pet him with her hands.

After their brushing ritual, Miranda and Butterscotch would play with his toys. In the beginning, they only had the toys that Jennifer had left for Butterscotch, and he was starting to lose interest in them. Bob and Miranda tried to keep adding to Butterscotch's toy collection, as he loved to play and seemed to get bored easily. One of the earliest toys that Miranda made for B. was a catnip-filled sock that had a hole poked in the toe. She would hold the sock over Butterscotch and shake the catnip out around and over him. As the particles of catnip fell on Butterscotch, he would wince, shiver, and run away. Miranda was surprised by Butterscotch's reaction, because she had always heard that cats love catnip. Miranda also took an empty toilet paper cardboard roll, cut holes in it, placed treats in it, and folded the ends over. She tried to get Butterscotch interested in this home-made toy as she had with the catnip-filled sock, but he didn't seem to know what to do with it.

As time went on, Bob bought plastic balls with bells inside, as well as rubber balls, and Butterscotch would swat at them and push them around as if they were mice. He would also play with the thin strip of polar fleece as if it was a snake.

Then Bob bought several new cat wands for Butterscotch's collection: one with feathers and bells; one with a catnip-filled bird with feathers; one with a ball and feathers; and one with a long fake fur snake. Butterscotch loved all of these wands—especially when Miranda would make the item on the end of the wand act like a prey animal and hide behind the door, another object, or higher up on a file cabinet. Another game that Miranda played with Butterscotch was leaving a treat under his door every night; sometimes he would push the treat back on her side of the door and she would have to keep pushing it back to him until he could get it. This became a nightly ritual with Butterscotch, as it would later with his friend, Gatsby too.

Bob and Miranda let their two meek and mild cocker spaniels, Spud and Ashley, come into Butterscotch's room to visit him. Butterscotch would try to nuzzle with, lick, and sniff them, but they would usually try to get away from him and eat the food in his food dish. After awhile, Miranda and Bob stopped inviting the dogs into Butterscotch's room, because they knew that the two dogs were only interested in eating his cat food.

Miranda figured that Butterscotch had to have been someone's pet, because he was very sweet to people and other animals, knew how to use a litter box, was an expert at playing with all kinds of cat toys, and loved eating dry cat kibble.

Jennifer's Visit with Butterscotch

When Jennifer would visit Butterscotch, he would lovingly lick her finger and she would thank him. Miranda said to Jennifer that he remembered that she was the person who rescued him from a hard life on the streets and brought him to live in their home with their family.

Miranda told Jennifer that their veterinarian, after looking at Butterscotch's teeth, estimated that he was five years old and she was surprised. On this visit, Jennifer brought a new toy for Butterscotch—it was another round toy with balls rolling around inside it with a plush bumble bee toy on top of it. Butterscotch instantly knew what to do with this toy as he did with the first one.

Then Miranda showed Jennifer a new toy advertised on television that they had just gotten for Butterscotch. It was a large fabric circle with a motorized mouse wand running underneath it at four different speeds.   Jennifer said that maybe she should get this toy for her cats. Miranda then told her that Butterscotch loved it and would play with it all day if she would let him.

Introduction to Gatsby

Bob was supposed to drive a kitten to a shelter for a transport, but the transport was cancelled. At the time, Miranda was inquiring about adopting this kitten, because Bob and she wanted to get a playmate for Butterscotch.

The shelter's personnel told Miranda that that particular cat would be better in a home as an only cat, but that there were some other very nice cats in the shelter that might be suitable playmates for Butterscotch.

Miranda described Butterscotch's mellow, easygoing personality and approximate age to Janine, a worker at the shelter, who was also a cat expert. She came up with a list of four or five cats who would be great matches for Butterscotch.

Miranda noticed that there was one female cat's name on the list, but she was later told that this cat acted more like a male than a female cat. Miranda was concerned about adding a female cat, because Jennifer had recommended that they get a male for Butterscotch to play with. She added that her female cat had bitten and scratched her and didn't get along that well with her male cats.

After reviewing the shelter's list of recommended playmates for Butterscotch, Bob and Miranda decided that Gatsby would be a good match. He was a nine-month-old, mild-mannered black-and-white "tuxedo" kitten.

Gatsby at the Shelter

Miranda had always wanted a dog named Gatsby, as it was similar to the name, Gumby. Years ago, they had had a dog named Gumby, but he had died. Miranda found it interesting that their Gatsby came to them in the form of a cat instead of a dog.

Gatsby, the Tuxedo Kitten

In an e-mail, Janine provided a detailed list of instructions for introducing cats to a household gradually in stages. Miranda was surprised, because she was not expecting a long and drawn-out process—she had thought that Bob and she could just put two cats together and they would be fine.

Before Bob brought Gatsby home, Miranda cat-proofed and cleaned their bathroom before his arrival. She set up a litter box and set out food and water dishes, as well as Butterscotch's cat tree for Gatsby. Once home, Bob brought the crate with Gatsby into the bathroom and opened the crate door. Gatsby then jumped up on the bathroom vanity and then up again higher to the top of the armoire where the cat tree was sitting. Gatsby went right into the carpeted cube and stayed there. From there, he had a very good view out of the bathroom window-- just like he used to have at the animal shelter where he had stayed. Miranda and Bob could tell that he was scared, though, and needed to get used to his new surroundings.

Gatsby's New Room—the Bathroom!

When Miranda would come to visit Gatsby, she would sit on the toilet, and he would come out of his cube to be petted and jump up on her lap. When bathing, she'd have to put Gatsby in his crate, so that he didn't get wet or in the way. After using the litter box, Gatsby would leave pieces of cat litter on the floor and it would stick to the floor when it got wet. Bob and Miranda could tell that Gatsby liked living in the bathroom, but they wanted their bathroom back!

While he lived in their bathroom, Miranda tried to get Gatsby interested in playing with toys. She rolled around one of Butterscotch's balls, but he showed no interest whatsoever in it. Miranda also introduced some of Butterscotch's toys to Gatsby, such as his bird and feather wands, but Gatsby hissed at the wands.

There was an incident late one night, where their dog, Speedy, and Miranda were awakened by what sounded like a big commotion in the bathroom. It stopped, so they went back to sleep. The next morning, Miranda found a dead mouse lying in their living room. There was no blood on the mouse, but Miranda suspected that Gatsby might have had something to do with its demise, so she went to check the bathroom, where she found the bathmat knocked down on the floor and the plug for the bathtub drain pulled out of its hole. It was starting to appear to Miranda that their innocent and harmless-looking Gatsby was a good mouser.

Miranda and Bob read in Janine's instructions that they should introduce the cats to each other's scents using a scent cloth and by exchanging their beds and rooms. Gatsby hissed at Butterscotch's bed and seemed to smell the scent cloth that Miranda had just rubbed on Butterscotch with little excitement or interest. In contrast, Butterscotch, when presented with Gatsby's scent cloth, would lick it affectionately. When Bob exchanged the cats' beds, Gatsby again hissed at Butterscotch's bed, but Miranda saw no reaction from Butterscotch when she placed Gatsby's bed in Butterscotch's room. In addition to the exchanging of the scent cloths and beds, both cats seemed to enjoy their times exploring things in the other cat's room.

The Cat Suite, a Dog-Free Zone

Bob and Miranda wanted to start moving Gatsby out of their bathroom, so Miranda asked Bob to create a "cat suite" out of their hallway, which could become a "dog-free zone" when all or most of the other doors were closed.

The Hallway Becomes the Cat Suite

They planned on installing three doors: one screen door on their bedroom, one screen door on Butterscotch's room, and one solid door at the hallway entrance, which could be locked from either side using sliding locks.

After Bob installed these three doors, Miranda moved a chair out into the hallway and had visits with Gatsby by closing all of the doors except the bathroom door. After a few days, Gatsby started venturing out of the bathroom and into the hallway to rub on her legs and jump up into her lap. Miranda would pet Gatsby for awhile, climb up on the shelves of the hallway bookcase, and then he would eventually return to the safety and security of the bathroom. These hallway visits went on for several days; then Miranda started opening up Butterscotch's screen door. Gatsby would run up to the door and hiss at Butterscotch, who never hissed at Gatsby. Miranda would also let Butterscotch come out into the hallway to explore and he would sniff and paw under Gatsby's closed bathroom door.

Gatsby Finally Becomes Butterscotch's Roommate

About one week later, Miranda and Bob moved Gatsby's litter box, food and water dishes, and the cat tree into Butterscotch's room. Gatsby would stay in the cube of the cat tree most of the time, except for when he ate, drank, or used the litter box.

Gatsby and Butterscotch—Together at Last

As a new cat owner, Miranda was delighted to see a marathon of the "My Cat from Hell" series with the cat expert, Jackson Galaxy, on Animal Planet. Jackson would offer tips on how to build a system of perches which he called a "cat superhighway." This system would enable cats to move all around a room at a level high off of the floor and confidently take charge of their space in a household. He also discussed how humans can sometimes inadvertently cause problems for cats and how they can solve the problems that arise.

At this time, Miranda was worried about whether their two cats would ever get along and if Gatsby would ever play with toys. Miranda was thankful that they did not experience the aggression, urination, and other behavioral problems with their cats that the cats on this cable television series had had.

As time went on, Gatsby stopped avoiding Butterscotch, as Butterscotch forced more opportunities for meeting and interacting by chasing Gatsby out of his cube. Gatsby went from avoiding to hissing at Butterscotch, until, eventually, all of the hissing ceased.

Miranda thought that Gatsby accepted Butterscotch as an older, more experienced cat, because Gatsby would step aside when Butterscotch tried to steal Gatsby's food. When Miranda would see that happening, though, she would chase Butterscotch away with the litter scoop. She also noticed that Butterscotch liked to chase down Gatsby and pull him into playful, non-aggressive, wrestling matches.

In one of her e-mails, Jennifer told Miranda that she had two feral cats that would fight and did not get along with each other, but Miranda did not think that this was the case with Butterscotch and Gatsby. Miranda saw Butterscotch and Gatsby showing physical affection toward each other, by grooming and licking each other. She also saw that when Gatsby had had enough of a wrestling match, he would jump up on the file cabinet and swat at Butterscotch through the bars of the chair that Butterscotch was sitting on. Miranda even witnessed Gatsby initiating a sparring match with Butterscotch, but that wasn't very often.

Eventually, Miranda was happy to report that Gatsby slowly started playing with the feather and other cat wands and the rabbit Kong Wubba toy. She figured that this was due to Gatsby's watching Butterscotch constantly playing with his toys and learning by imitation.

In order for the two cats to not feel too trapped and to stretch their legs, Miranda would let them out into the hallway with all of the other doors closed. There were times when Gatsby and Butterscotch were at their screen door asking to be let out, but she did not let them out all of the time. Miranda tried walking both Butterscotch and Gatsby on leashes around the house at different times, but they both were able to jump up and out of their collars and harnesses, so she decided to abandon that idea.

New Cat Toys

In order to save money, Miranda first decided to try out with their cats some of their dogs' toys that they do not play with anymore. Butterscotch and Gatsby did not seem to like the burlap bag that barked or the ball that talked, but there were several toys that they liked.

One dog toy that was a big hit with their cats was a round wooden treat dispenser with cubbyholes and doors with knobs or hinges that could be opened with the swipe of a paw. Luckily, there was one open space in the toy, where Miranda would put a treat for Butterscotch. She showed Butterscotch how to open the knobs and doors of this treat toy many times, but he did not catch on. Gatsby, on the other hand, caught on to it right away, so he was able to get four treats for every one treat that Butterscotch got. To even things up, if Gatsby forgot to take a treat out of a cubbyhole, Miranda would give that treat to Butterscotch.

Another type of dog toy that Bob's and Miranda's cats liked was the squeaking toy in the forms of a squirrel, mouse, and bird. Still another dog toy adopted by Butterscotch and Gatsby was the Kong Wubba, the gray rabbit toy mentioned earlier. Miranda would make it squeak and then she would throw it towards Butterscotch or Gatsby, who proceeded to bite or lick the head while clawing it with their back feet.

Besides these dog toys, Bob bought some cat toys, two of which glowed in the dark. The two cats usually just stared at the laser light toy, but Butterscotch had chased the laser points in the past when he was in the mood. Miranda felt that she had to turn off this toy, though, when Butterscotch would stand in front of it, because she did not want him looking directly into the laser light and burning his retinas.

Bob recently added a wand that has a mouse that squeaks and has flashing lights for eyes when the wand is bumped against something. Butterscotch liked this wand and wanted to attack the mouse; whereas, Gatsby would just stare at it and watch the mouse while it squeaked and its eyes flashed at him. Added at this time also were two toy mice that squeaked when bumped.

Besides the squeaking mouse wand and the two squeaking mice toys, Miranda ordered the cat toy called "Batting Practice," which was a squeaking and flashing mouse attached to a rope that hangs from a door. The cats loved swinging at the mouse to make it squeak, but one morning, she found it lying on the floor. Luckily, Miranda was able to fit the rope attachment back into its hinge on top of the door and the toy was useable once again. Miranda noticed that Butterscotch liked getting up on top of one of the file cabinets, as it made swiping at the mouse with his paw a whole lot easier. She also noticed that he liked playing with these toys at night, because she would hear the toy mice squeaking at 3:00 A.M.

Conclusion

Before their experiences with Butterscotch and Gatsby, Miranda and Bob did not know much if anything about cats. They learned that when adopting your first and multiple cats, it is a wise practice to:

a) Consult with cat experts;
b) For your second cat, ask for a cat that is compatible in temperament with your first one. Because Gatsby was a meek, nine-month-old kitten, he was less likely to fight with Butterscotch, who was a much older and experienced adult cat. Bob and Miranda were told that an older cat might have challenged and fought with Butterscotch over food and territory.
c) Introduce your new cat to your first cat gradually;
d) Cats are captive animals. It is a good idea to keep getting your cats new toys to keep them entertained, so that they are not missing being out in the wild, hunting, and prowling;
e) Miranda figured that by having two indoor cats who would probably eat three animals per day, they are saving about two thousand, one hundred ninety wild birds, mice, squirrels, chipmunks, rabbits, and other small animals per year from terrible deaths;
f) By keeping these two cats indoors, Miranda and Bob are not only saving their cats' lives and protecting them from diseases, bad weather, and predators, but they are preventing their cats from producing many unwanted litters out in the wild..

ANTON'S JOURNEY ON THE ABOVE-GROUND RAILROAD

Introduction to Anton

Miranda first learned of Anton, an eight-month-old hound mix puppy from Alabama, when his photo and information were sent to Bob and Miranda in a cross-posted e-mail from Becky, an animal transport coordinator for whom Bob had driven dogs in the past. In his picture portrait, Anton was wearing a bow-tie collar and looked adorable.

Worried about Anton, Miranda sent an e-mail to Debbie at Anton's shelter saying that they would be willing to adopt him outright if Debbie got no replies. Miranda told Debbie that they have been adopting animals whom no one else wants, like their Buster, who would have just sat in a rescue facility. Debbie mentioned that there was a rescue that would take Anton, but adoption for Anton was preferred to going to a rescue, as he had been through so much!

Anton's story was a tragic one. Anton, his siblings, and another shelter dog named Hermes, all caught distemper. While Anton was lying down next to his sister, Irma, and Hermes, who both lay dying, three different vets recommended that Anton also be euthanized. Anton's front legs were starting to give out on him and he was falling face-down on the floor, but two weeks after being given a special serum treatment by his foster mother, Anu, Anton's legs started working again.

Miraculously, Anton survived. This serum method was discovered by a California veterinarian, and his foster mother, Anu, asked her own veterinarian in Alabama to mix it for her using his clinic's centrifuge. She said, "Anton has smiled at the face of death and survived...the antibiotics are so important for these pups."

Anton was left with some side effects of the distemper—he salivated a lot and his head bobbed involuntarily, but the disease did not take away his sweetness, loveable qualities, or his intelligence. Miranda knew that Anton was intelligent, because she saw him change direction in midstream while his new pal, Lucky, was chasing him.

Indeed, Anton was still a normal puppy who liked to bark, chew up things, play with, and chase his new pack members on the trails at his new home. In fact, Miranda observed that Anton's head-bobbing and salivating symptoms seemed to actually lessen or abate when he was busy playing or running with his other pack members, and she surmised that it probably was a nice respite for Anton, albeit a short one, from those pesky symptoms.

Next on Anton's to-do list was learning obedience and leash training. Also, he was quite thin, so Miranda and Bob wanted to see him gain some weight. He liked the food that they gave him, so they figured that he wouldn't have trouble gaining a few pounds on his very thin frame.

It was a welcome breakthrough when Anton and Lucky, their two-year-old husky-shepherd mix, became friends and started playing with each other; it had taken them some time to warm up to each other.

Bob and Miranda Become Involved in Transports

Several years before, Bob and Miranda became aware that there were in-state and inter-state animal transports going on each weekend all over the country, and they wanted to become involved. The two of them started their adventure into animal rescue with Bob driving and hosting the dogs over-night and with Miranda watching transports on the weekdays and e-mailing back and forth with offers to the transport coordinators while caring for and watching their own pets.

These transports usually originated in the southern states and would go all of the way up to rescues in Minnesota. Miranda's and Bob's cottage was situated near the transport route that a lot of the transports use, so Bob was soon driving for one or more transports every weekend.

Usually Bob and Miranda were the volunteers transporting for others, but in this particular instance, their new dog, Anton, would be driven and hosted overnight on their behalf by many other drivers in one of these transports.

How Transports Work

A transport like this begins with one or more shelters that are called, "sending rescues." These sending rescues have contacted "receiving rescues," the shelters that are going to take in, care for, and find homes for the animals; these animals are specific dogs and cats who are non-aggressive and who have been "vetted"—that is, seen a vet for a basic check-up and immunizations. These rescues—both sending and receiving—are reputable and have been checked out beforehand to make sure that they treat animals humanely. This has to be done, because the animals could end up in the hands of abusive or cruel people who just call themselves rescues in order to get dogs for such terrible practices as fighting or medical experimentation.

After the receiving rescues agree to take in specific animals, the transport coordinator can compose and send out a run sheet to solicit volunteer drivers, some of whom are working at the sending and receiving rescues. It is a common practice for a person from the sending rescue to drive the first leg and a person from the receiving rescue to drive the last leg of the transport to get things going and encourage others to drive for the transport.

A run sheet consists of a number of fifty-to-one hundred mile legs that are to be driven by one or more drivers, depending upon the total number of passengers for that weekend's transport. Passengers are listed in a numbered sequence on the run sheet, and the same types of information are listed for each passenger.

Anton's Transport

Two drivers were needed for each leg of Anton's transport, which had twenty legs. The first leg started in Birmingham, Alabama and the last leg ended in Isle, Minnesota. Anton was listed as Passenger #10. Just as there was information listed for the other passengers, there was information listed for Anton. It included: Breed (Hound mix); Age (8 months); Gender (male); Size/Weight (40 lbs.); Spayed/Neutered (yes); General Temperament (very sweet and friendly); Any Special Needs (none); Items Provided (medical records, health certificate); Crate (not provided); Reason for Transport (rescue to approved adopter); Vaccines (UTD—dh2pp, rabies).

There were nine other passengers on this transport's run sheet, with other passengers allowed to be added on later.

Anton met Bob at leg number fifteen in Milwaukee. Bob drove Anton along with some added-on passengers and the passengers listed for his leg on the run sheet.

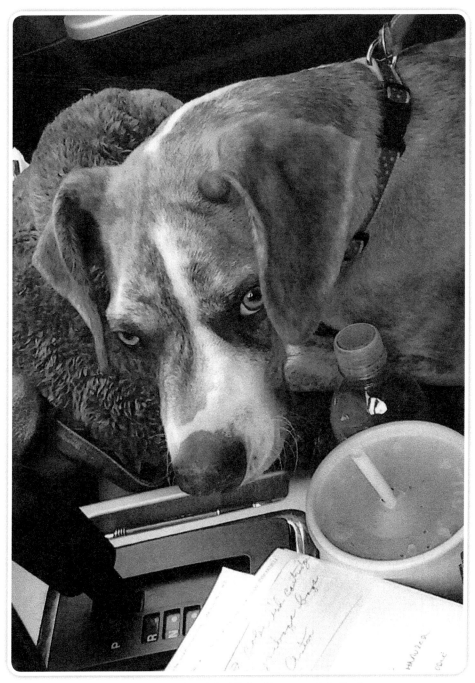

Anton Begins His Ride Home with Bob

He dropped off the added-on passengers in Delafield and the other passengers in Madison; then he took Anton to Miranda's and Bob's home to become part of their pack.

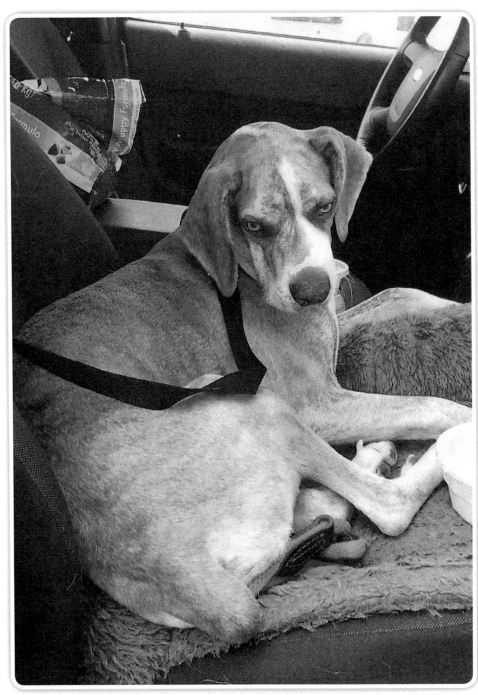

Anton Enjoys the Scenery on the Ride to His New Home

Anton is Safe and Sound in His New Bed

Other Facts about Animal Rescue Transports

The transport coordinator plugs in drivers' names on the run sheet as they volunteer to drive particular legs of the transport. As it gets closer to the start of the transport, the coordinator updates the run sheet and sends out an e-mail listing the legs where drivers are still needed. Usually there is a deadline date and time for accepting drivers, so coordinators get nervous as the deadline approaches. Often, the coordinators will use the words, "begging, desperate, failing transport, etc." in the subject lines of their e-mails to get the attention of prospective drivers.

While a transport is going on, the dogs get a bathroom and water break and one driver of each leg calls the coordinator to report on any problems during the hand-offs of their passengers. Drivers will give the coordinator traffic and weather reports, as well as health or behavioral issues concerning the animals, such as if two dogs are not getting along and need to be separated or if the puppies need to be given extra water. Then the coordinator posts this information in e-mails to everyone on her transport list. Currently, most transport coordinators are female, but drivers are both males and females.

Some one-day transports occur on a Friday or Saturday, but many other transports start early on Saturday and end late on Sunday. This was the case with Anton's transport, which started at 7:30 AM on Saturday and ended at 10:45 PM on Sunday. Such two-day and three-day transports require that the passengers stay over-night at someone's house for one or two nights. For Anton's transport, there were four people hosting six dogs and two puppies at their homes in or around Indianapolis, Indiana.

Animals have to be driven to the point where a transport begins, so sometimes a foster person or shelter person will do this driving to get the animals to where they have to be to join the transport.

When puppies are transported, the abbreviation "NPOG" is used. It stands for no paws on ground. Because they are too young to have shots, they are susceptible to catching fatal diseases like parvovirus, if their paws touch the ground and they then lick their paws. Viruses like parvovirus are known to survive in the ground for six months, so an infected site is a real danger for puppies that are being transported. There are notices that some coordinators send around to the drivers on their lists warning that some sites are contaminated; in those cases, the coordinators will change the drop-off and pick-up locations until those sites are deemed safe again.

Puppies are very cute, but they can be very messy—vomit, urine, and stool are common on puppies, in crates, and in cars. Drivers will often bring cleaning supplies with them to clean up the puppies, the crates, and the carpeting in their vehicles. Some transports encourage the drivers to have Pedia Lyte on hand for puppies, so that they do not get dehydrated in hot weather.

A run sheet lists the following for each leg: the starting city and state to the next city and state, the number of miles and the duration of the trip, the start time and end time, and the drivers' names. Some coordinators include a meeting place for pick-ups and drop-offs on the run sheet; whereas, other coordinators leave it up to the drivers to contact the drivers before and after them to set up a meeting place. McDonalds and other fast food restaurants are examples of sites where pick-ups and drop-offs regularly take place.

Dogs and cats are transported by the out-of-state transports. In-state transports can include animals besides dogs and cats. They can carry birds, farm animals, snakes, ferrets, lizards, and other animals. One time, Bob transported some tarantulas for a Wisconsin transport group. The drivers for these in-state transports don't always know who is going to be riding with them on their next transport!

On out-of-state and in-state transports, medical papers have to be handed off from driver to driver. That is the law!

Cross-posting is a term which means that a person can't drive a transport leg themselves, but they can send an e-mail including a coordinator's needs to people on their e-mail lists.

Some run sheets include photos of passengers, while some do not.

When a driver signs up to drive for a new coordinator, they are asked to provide such information as: name, address, cell phone number, e-mail address, references, car brand, color, and license number, and the number of passengers that they can carry. Also, there are transport rules that the driver is required to read, such as not to bring your own children or animals along with you on transports and not to remove an animal from a transport.

A transport's routes are pretty well-established, but the coordinator may later choose to change the location of a stop, due to a lack of drivers, a parvovirus outbreak at the site, to avoid tolls, or some other valid reason.

Drivers often need to provide their own crates and tethers, and they need to figure out the number and sizes of crates to load into their vehicles beforehand. Every animal on a transport should be viewed as a potential flight risk. For that reason, strong slip leads, leashes, and double tethers should be used—especially for large and powerful breeds--to ensure that the dogs do not escape and get hit by a car or truck on the freeway. Such things have happened during transports, so one can never be too careful.

Vans are definitely an advantage in transports, because they can take twice as many or more animals as a car or sports utility vehicle. For legs that are having trouble being filled, a van can eliminate the need for one extra driver and save an entire transport.

All personnel involved are necessary for a transport to take place, whether they are from a rescue, driving, hosting animals overnight, or coordinating. Without any one of these key links, the transport can be in danger of failing.

Anton's Fairytale Ending

Bob and Miranda were amazed when Becky, the transport coordinator, said that Anton has a fan club, or following, of about forty drivers who like to receive regular updates on his progress.

Sweet Dreams for Anton

They were so happy that transports exist--like the one that helped Anton. Homes are waiting for these needy dogs, cats, and other animals, and their futures depend on their getting to their destinations.

These transports are like a modern-day underground railroad—only they are for animals instead of humans. It is a wonderful way of saving homeless animals that have been dumped in shelters with high-kill rates!

If you are interested in driving for transports, Miranda urges you to go online and sign up for one that goes through or within your state. She says that it is very rewarding and that you won't regret it!

Anton's Legacy You Tube Videos on Curing Distemper and Saving Dogs

If you are interested in saving dogs that have contracted distemper, please view Anton's foster mother, Anu's Distemper Don't Kill videos:

Distemper Don't Kill (Anton's Legacy); Distemper Don't Kill – Day By Day (Anton's Legacy); Distemper Don't Kill – Day 1 (Anton's Legacy); Distemper, Treatment and Hope; Distemper, Anton's and Emily's Legacy; Copy of Distemper Babies Making Themselves Right at Home (Anton's Legacy); A New (Anu) Protocol for Animal Shelters (Anton 's Legacy); Through Hermes Came Solutions; Signs of Life; Diet; Treatment & Timing.

The Beginning of a Dog Park

Miranda and Bob have their own backyard dog park. It is situated on one and one-half acres of beautiful, forested land. It all started when Bob mowed a basic circular trail in 1997. They walked with their deceased dogs, Chewy, a husky-German Shepherd mix, Gilligana, a black Halden hound, and Lizzie, their buff Cocker Spaniel, on that trail for twelve years, and it stayed the same until 2013.

Lizzie would always take the same shortcut to meet them at a particular spot on the trail. At first, they joked about it, but finally, Bob mowed it and it became known as "Lizzie's Shortcut." Other shortcuts evolved over time as Miranda or the dogs created them by walking. These shortcuts were also named after Miranda's and Bob's different dogs. There was Chewy's shortcut, which led to the birdfeeder area, Daisy's shortcut, which led from the back woodpile, Gilligana's run, where she used to play Frisbee with Bob, Spud's shortcut, which started at the trail head, Maverick's shortcut, which went past the picnic table, and Speedy's shortcut--the shortest one of all, which led from the picnic area to the side wood pile.

New shortcuts continued to be born as Miranda later discovered two un-mowed shortcuts that the dogs had created through their repeated walking and which they all were regularly using anyway. Miranda decided to name one Ashley's shortcut, because Ashley regularly used it and the other one Buster's shortcut, because he would get fatigued and was constantly short-cutting during the entire trail walk anyway.

How the Trail Evolved Into a Dog Park

In 2013, Bob and Miranda made some major improvements to their trail:

1) Bob cut down a large dead tree, as well as two smaller trees to make room for an added trail section on the east side of our backyard. This land had previously been left out of the trail, so Bob cleared and mowed it to enlarge the overall trail.

2) On weekends during the whole summer, Bob put up a wire fence with wooden posts around the outside perimeter of the entire trail, along with three gates—one near the back woodpile, and two on either side of the house.

3) During this time, Bob and Miranda had to fight off mosquitoes, biting flies, and

pesky gnats, which were merciless during the slow process of post-digging and wire hanging and fastening.

How the Dogs Liked the Dog Park

The dogs seemed to like leaving waste piles in and along the trail, even though Miranda and Bob let them go into the latrine beforehand. The latrine was a fenced-in area with dirt and leaves that the dogs could go to from the back door of the house and down the porch steps. The dogs also liked to toilet on the shorter trail loops. When Bob or Miranda saw a pile, they would flick it off into the bushes using a stick.

Every day, Miranda would usually walk the trail before anyone else to maintain it. Examples of things that she found on her "maintenance walks" included: a large tree lying across the trail or the top of the fence, heavy or light tree branches, dead birds, sticks, encroaching thorny plants, weeds, tree roots, stones, acorns, bark pieces that had been stripped off of trees by pileated woodpeckers, and piles of dog waste.

Older dogs like Buster liked to take the shortcuts and rejoin Miranda and Ashley on the trail as if they had been walking the entire distance for the whole time with us.

Miranda would walk six circuits around the outside trail each day. In the beginning, she would walk eighteen circuits which equaled one mile before the trail was enlarged. As her life became busier, Miranda found that she had to reduce her overall time spent walking on the trail.

Miranda noticed that the larger, younger, and more playful dogs liked to run and chase each other without regard for the safety of the slower, older walkers on the trail. The younger dogs were knocking over and jumping over the older dogs. This was a real hazard, so Miranda and Bob decided to walk their dogs in four shifts that were more appropriate in age and size.

First, the smaller, older dogs would walk. They included: Spud, Ashley, Buster, and Rusty. Then Lucky, the big dog, would run loose and play fetch with Bob. Then the medium-sized dogs, Maverick and Speedy, would get to run with and chase each other. Finally, the large dogs, Daisy and Anton would run free while Bob walked a somewhat tired Lucky on the leash.

Lucky Playing With Anton

Maverick Playing with Speedy

When Miranda would let the dogs out of the gate, they were always very excited to the point of crawling over each other, and then they would run out and sound like galloping horses. During the day, the dogs would keep reminding Miranda that they wanted to go out on the trails and that it was the highlight of their day. They would start squealing and jumping up on Miranda and each other whenever they saw her outside-shoes on her feet and heard the jingling of her keys.

Miranda noticed that the dogs would walk in sub-packs and follow their favorite human. For example, Ashley would go wherever her best friend, Spud, would go. Also, Bob's younger and more energetic dogs would walk and play with him on the trail; whereas, Miranda's older and slower dogs would walk with her on the trail.

In the summer, Bob and Miranda would put out a water bowl on the porch during the trail walks. Usually Miranda would have to refill it, because their big dog, Lucky, would drink up one whole bowl by himself.

Hazards to Watch Out For

Miranda was very happy to have this fence erected, because they had had a parade of stray animals, two Doberman Pinchers, 1 German Shepherd, 1 Pit Bull Terrier, and two other dogs roaming cross their property, as well as cats, skunks, raccoons, deer, possums, ground hogs, and turkeys. She didn't want any of their dogs, especially Maverick, to get into an altercation with, or try to chase, one of these animals.

Miranda still worried about the hawks that visited their yard periodically and ambushed birds that were feeding at their birdfeeders. She was afraid to have their little dogs, Buster and Rusty, outside when she heard the hawks' cries. Miranda had read previously about a hawk picking up a dachshund (Rusty) and then dropping him when he got too heavy. She also read that this caused a lot of medical problems for the dachshund who had been attacked by the hawk.

Bob had to make special fencing above and below their porches to prevent their dogs from escaping. He also fenced in their garden to keep their dogs out of it. Some of the dogs had already caught on to the "holes" in the fencing, so the special fencing had to be done soon afterwards.

The latrine fence wire was not as tall or as strong as that of the trail fence wire. Bob and Miranda had had a break-in through the back door of the house about a year before, and the burglar had bent down some of the latrine wire while he was scaling it. The trail fence, which was outside of the latrine fence, was good to have as a further protection against the dogs' escaping if they were able to dig themselves out of or jump over their latrine.

A farmer owned the land behind Miranda's and Bob's dog park. One week, a property surveyor company had placed bright pink flags on posts and pink and green tapes around trees back there on the farmer's land. Bob and Miranda were not sure how this surveying would affect their dog park. They were not sure if people, cows, or hunters would be walking near their back fence, so they planned on having Bob erect a privacy fence along that corridor if that were to happen. This privacy fence would help keep their dogs safe during their walks, as well as keep their dogs from interacting with the humans or animals on the other side of the fence.

Bob and Miranda could tell that their dogs preferred to be off-leash, run around freely, and walk at their own pace. When one of their dogs was acting too wildly, chasing squirrels up trees, or wouldn't come inside the house when they were called (Buster, Maverick, Speedy), then they would be put back on-leash (Maverick). Bob had tried walking their dogs at the dog park back in Milwaukee, but Maverick was always trying to play with the humans instead of the other dogs, and the people were getting cranky with him and telling him to go away.

Some of Miranda's and Bob's dogs liked to dig holes in the latrine (Lucky/Anton), and some liked to dig holes on the trails (Maverick). Where there were chipmunk holes, some of the dogs would stick their noses (Maverick) or entire faces (Lucky) into the holes. Miranda would discourage them from doing this when she saw this behavior, as she didn't want them to be bitten.

Also, Miranda would keep finding small holes dug up on the trail, and the soil was soft enough that she could rub them out with her foot. She was worried that the dogs could trip and fall if they stuck their feet in these holes while they were running and chasing on the trails.

In addition, Speedy and Maverick were sniffing at a point at the back fence, where there was a depression in the dirt from some digging done on the other side of the fence. Evidently, a wild animal was trying to get into the dog park. This wasn't hard to believe, as a number of wild animals lost their access to that land and their birdfeeders when the dog park fence was erected. These wild animals included: raccoons, deer, skunks, possums, rabbits, ground hogs, and turkeys.

One of the things that Miranda worried about most was that a tree could fall on all or any of them while they were walking on the trails. There were many dead mature trees on their property, and in the past, trees had been brought down by wind storms. There were times that Bob and Miranda were outside or even inside their house when they heard a tree or tree branch fall down. It was quite loud and sometimes it would shake the house with the vibrations made by its impact with the ground or other trees. Unfortunately Miranda and Bob were not in a position to be able to hire someone to cut down these trees, so they had to take their chances until they could afford to hire a tree service.

There was an instance, though, where Bob and Miranda were able to "make lemons out of lemonade." A very large and heavy tree had fallen, and it was so heavy that Bob couldn't move it and had to leave it on the trail. When they would pass by the log on the trail, Maverick and Speedy started jumping up on the log to get a better view of things around them. Eventually Miranda trained some of their other medium-sized dogs (Spud, Ashley) to jump up on the log as well. They called it their "Agility Log." There was a smaller piece of the log that jutted out from the base of the log on the right side and since it wasn't so tall, Miranda encouraged her smaller, older dogs (Buster, Rusty) to climb up on that piece.

Speedy and Maverick on the Agility Log

Another opportunity for climbing exercise during the trail walk was the side porch steps. Miranda noticed that after each circuit that they completed, Ashley would climb up the porch steps indicating that she wanted to go into the house. Other dogs started to follow her as well and they would all be waiting for Miranda to let them in through the door. Instead, Miranda told them that they weren't done and that they needed to come down the steps and walk some more. Miranda didn't mind this, because she felt that the dogs were getting good stair climbing exercise when they did this between each circuit around the trail.

Ashley Climbs the Porch Steps

When Bob's and Miranda's dogs would go off of the cleared trails, they would encounter thorny brambles from time to time. Miranda would try to remind them to stay on the trails, but they didn't always listen to her. On one walk, Miranda heard Buster squeak after walking into a plant that seemed to grab him with its thorny tentacles. Thankfully, they didn't seem to have problems with poison ivy or getting hit by acorns that would fall hard on the surfaces that they hit.

On other walks, Miranda would watch the dogs to see that they didn't eat wild berries, mushrooms, or dead birds. One day, she caught Rusty trying to wolf down the remains of a red-headed woodpecker. Luckily, she caught him in time and he regurgitated it. Then she was able to dispose of it, so that another dog wouldn't be able to eat it, as dogs can get worms from eating the carcasses of dead birds or other animals.

Still at other times, Miranda noticed that some of their dogs would snap at and try to eat yellow jackets or flies (Daisy, Maverick, and Lucky). Maverick was stung on the front of his neck after snapping at a yellow jacket, and he had a huge, red, angry welt. Yellow jackets were very plentiful on their property and Miranda figured that they must have a nest nearby.

Miranda and Bob had not spent their first winter with the dog park yet, but they figured that winter on the trails would be very difficult, as they would need to snow-blown by Bob. Shoveling the long trail would be a very difficult-to-impossible job—especially if the snow was heavy and wet.

Conclusion

Miranda and Bob felt that their dog park was a great success because:

1) It was the closest thing to freedom for their pets, who were "captive animals";

2) It gave their dogs good exercise and tired them out, so that they weren't too wild or irritable in their house and they slept well;

3) They didn't have to make daily trips to the local dog park—it was right outside their back door;

4) All of their dogs knew each other. This served to reduce the likelihood of fights and lawsuits, which are common fare on the court television shows.

One day when their cat expert, Jennifer, was visiting their cat Butterscotch, Miranda invited Jennifer to walk on the new trails with her. Miranda told her that a backyard dog park has both advantages and disadvantages. She added, "It has changed our dogs' lives as well as our own; it is probably not for everyone, but we sure appreciate having it. If I had to describe my idea of heaven, this dog park would be it!"

Doggy Heaven

THEIR UNSUNG DOGS

Introduction

Miranda was convinced that no dog, cat, or other animal was ordinary. Although some of their dogs didn't have enough material about them to write an entire story, Miranda wanted, as a tribute to their unsung dogs, to mention what it was that made each of these dogs special.

Pooky

Pooky was Miranda's and Bob's first dog that they had as a married couple. She was a medium-sized black German shepherd and Labrador mix that they got as a puppy from their local humane society.

Pooky was very sweet, easy-going, and an avid Frisbee player. She liked to urinate behind their chairs and couch, but that was as mischievous as she got.

She developed a large cancerous tumor at the base of her tail and had it removed. The tumor grew back, though, and Pooky had the second tumor removed also. The skin near her tail was pulled tightly from the second tumor removal and Pooky seemed to be in pain. She would come to Miranda who was sitting at her desk, whine, and put her head on Miranda's leg. Eventually, the tumor affected Pooky's back legs and she couldn't walk.

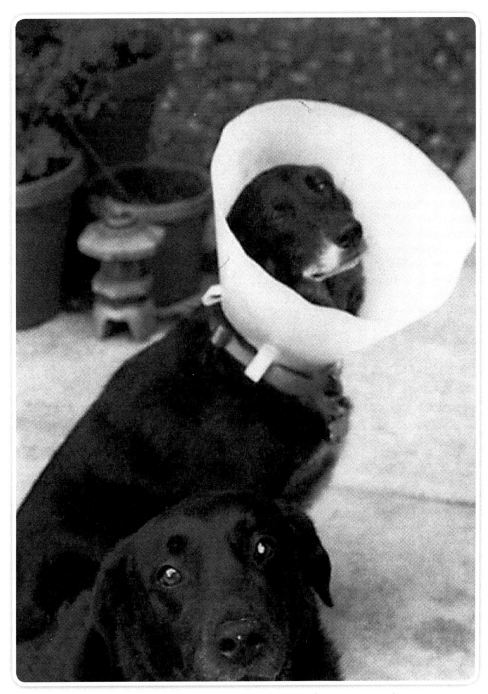

Pooky Wearing a Cone after One of Her Surgeries

Gumby

Bob and Miranda got Gumby as a playmate for Pooky. When they chose Gumby's name, Miranda and Bob were trying to make their names sound like the cartoon series, "Pokey and Gumby." Gumby was also a very easy dog to have for Bob and Miranda as first-time dog-owners. He was a short, stocky, and muscular black Labrador mix. Gumby was quiet, unassuming, and loved to eat. They could tell that he had a sense of smell that was even more developed than the average dog, because his nose seemed to lead him to any food that was in the vicinity.

Pooky and Gumby Napping on a Chair Together

Eventually, Gumby developed cataracts in both eyes and went blind, but he insisted on walking up and down the steps of the house. In a new house that they were having built, Gumby leaned over a railing-less basement that was full of water and fell into the water with a very loud splash.

Bob then rushed down the steps to rescue Gumby. He lifted Gumby out of the water and carried a very heavy, wet dog up the steps. Luckily, the water had broken Gumby's fall and saved his life; he was un-hurt.

Miranda and Bob realized how lucky they were that the water was still in the basement and had not yet been pumped out; if the water had been pumped out of the basement, and the cement floor had been poured, Gumby would have been killed and it would have been a great tragedy.

Gilligana

Gilligana was supposed to be a male puppy, because Miranda's cousin, Connie, had promised them a male puppy and they were going to name him Gilligan after the bumbling and not-so-bright character from the "Gilligan's Island" television show. Connie's dog had just had a litter of puppies in her garage. She told them that they would get first pick of the litter, but it did not work out that way.

A few days later, though, they were told that the mother dog was hiding her puppies in the forest near her house and that they had better come quickly if they wanted to have one of those puppies. When Bob and Miranda arrived, Connie took them deep into the forest, where they listened for the yelps of any remaining puppies.

They found a puppy buried and crying under some leaves—this was the last and only puppy that they could find. This puppy was a female, so they took her home with them and named her "Gilligana" instead of the masculine form of the name, "Gilligan." Miranda enjoyed it when people would laugh as they heard her name, and the name, Gilligana, actually fit her quite well. She wasn't very smart, but she excelled as the household's athlete.

Gilligana as a Puppy, Chewing on a Corn Husk

As she grew up, she looked like a sleek black Labrador with a shiny coat and a muscular build. Miranda said that she should have known that Gilligana would become a great athlete, because the puppy would never stay on Miranda's lap long enough for her to pet her. Miranda thought something was wrong, because "Gilli" would keep running away to go outside and didn't want to be a lap dog. It turned out that Gilligana liked playing Frisbee and ball outside with Bob for hours on end. They figured that she would have played all day with him if they would have let her.

Gilligana, the Consummate Athlete

Another healthy habit that Gilligana had was that of eating fruits and vegetables. Gilli would eat apples, potatoes, broccoli, and other foods. Bob and Miranda had never had a dog who liked these foods—their dogs usually preferred eating meat. They figured that Gilli's healthy habits helped her to live to the age of fifteen, which was a good age for a dog of her size.

The only negative thing that they found about Gilli was that at times, she would act like a wild dog and bite their other dogs. At one time, she bit and tore Chewy's ear and nose, causing them to bleed and need first aid; another time, she bit Lizzie's face, causing a permanent scar during a fight over food; still yet another time, Gilli attacked Gumby, who was blind at the time, in her sleep when he accidentally stumbled into her. It occurred to Miranda that being hidden in a forest with the threat of being attacked by such animals as raccoons or coyotes might have caused Gilli to suffer from post-traumatic stress syndrome and, perhaps, flashbacks.

Lucky

Bob and Miranda heard of Barry's plight through an urgent e-mail sent out by an Illinois kill shelter. He was going to be killed soon, because the shelter didn't have any more room for him. The shelter later sent them a follow-up e-mail saying that there had been no offers to rescue Barry (soon to be re-named as Lucky), so Miranda responded with an offer to adopt and transport him. Miranda completed the adoption application with vet references and sent it to the shelter. That Saturday, Bob picked up Barry in Dubuque and brought him home.

A Happy Lucky Going Home

Miranda and Bob called him "Lucky," because he was lucky and had cheated death. He was a beautiful white Siberian Husky-German Shepherd mix with pretty brown eyes who reminded Miranda of their deceased husky-shepherd mix, Chewy. They soon saw that he was a two-year-old fifty-pound puppy who loved to run and chase their other dogs on the trails in their backyard dog park.

At first, two of their dogs were showing their teeth and charging at Lucky over rawhide bones. Miranda surmised that it was because he was larger than they were. Eventually, though, the challenges subsided and everyone seemed to get along.

Lucky was affectionate, and liked to sit up and put his paws on Miranda while she petted him. He also loved to chew and eat, and enjoyed doing outside doggie activities like chasing after a ball, digging holes, and lying in the dirt.

He was an "every dog," just an average dog that caught a very lucky break—hence the name, "Lucky." After adopting a parade of rescue dogs who could be called difficult due to their various behavioral and elimination problems, Lucky's simplicity was a breath of fresh air for Bob and Miranda. It was like having their first uncomplicated dogs, Pooky and Gumby, all over again!

Conclusion

Miranda's and Bob's dogs were each special in some way. Miranda wrote this chapter to honor those dogs of theirs that didn't have long or complicated stories to tell; yet the combination of their personalities and experiences were unique to them and she wanted their stories told.

Afterword

Our animals are, and will continue to be, our best friends until we die. It is our wish that you, the readers, can have such wonderful and interesting friends as Bob and I have had. Animal ownership is indeed a privilege.

If you do not have a companion animal and would like to add a new friend with which to share your life, we recommend that you adopt one from a rescue group or shelter.

Just like humans, each animal possesses an individual personality, and just like it is with having a baby, we believe that adopting an animal will positively change and enrich your life forever.

Miranda McAdams

Printed in the United States
By Bookmasters